1890~1920 America Becomes a World Power

Written by NAUNERLE FARR

Edited by D'ANN CALHOUN

Illustrated by RESTY RONGUILLO

Editorial consultant LAWRENCE W. BLOCH

A VINCENT FAGO PRODUCTION

Pendulum Press, Inc.

West Haven, Connecticut

ISBN 0-88301-199-9

Published by
PENDULUM PRESS, INC.
An Academic Industries, Inc., Company
The Academic Building
Saw Mill Road
West Haven, Connecticut 06516

Printed in the United States of America

To the Teacher:

With educators everywhere concerned about the literacy of the nation's children, attention has been focused primarily on the reading curriculum. Reading teachers can select from literally thousands of varied programs for their classes. Yet social studies teachers, faced with an equal amount of material to cover, are often at a loss. Although many history texts are available, they all seem to offer information alone at the expense of motivation. Out of this understanding the **Basic Illustrated History of America** series was developed.

Motivation is the basic premise and the outstanding strength of these texts. Each book was written in the belief that children will learn and remember whatever they find enjoyable. Through illustration, they are drawn into the reading matter, and learning begins.

Besides motivating, the illustrations provide clues to the meanings of words. Unfamiliar vocabulary is defined in footnotes. Every volume in the series has been edited to simplify the reading. And, since the interest level extends as far as the adult reader, students in all grades—even in remedial classes—will enjoy these texts. Finally, companion student activity books guide the reading with vocabulary drills and exercises on comprehension.

The **Basic Illustrated History of America** series, then, offers a new concept in the teaching of American history, yet one which does not subordinate content to form. Meticulously researched historical data provides the authenticity for costumes and architecture in each era. Together, the features of this unique series will make learning an enjoyable experience for the student—and a rewarding one for the teacher.

The editors

contents

Both France and Spain had hoped to build up their colonies in America. But in the Louisiana Purchase Napoleon sold his French lands to the United States. The Spanish colonies in South America then won their freedom. At that time these new nations were still young and weak. Therefore, in 1823, President Monroe announced the Monroe Doctrine. This warned that there could be no new colonies in either North or South America.

In 1863, Napoleon III, Emperor of France, sent a French army into Mexico.

The United States was fighting the Civil War. Secretary of State Seward talked with President Lincoln.

After helping the South in every way he could, Napoleon has now taken over Mexico!

This is clearly against the Monroe Doctrine. He counts on it that we are too busy with the South to fight France.

Which is true. Try to get word to the Mexicans that we have not forgotten them. After we have won the war, we will take action.

Napoleon made an Austrian nobleman, Maximilian, the Emperor* of Mexico. With his wife Carlota he went there.

In Mexico, Maximilian and Carlota were crowned.

I have been told that the Mexican people wish me to rule them!

You will be a fine emperor!

the ruler of a country and all its colonies

When the Civil War ended, the United States rushed 50,000 soldiers to the Mexican border. They would see that the Monroe Doctrine was kept.

In France, Louis Napoleon was angry.

Those Americans! Bring the French soldiers home from Mexico!

The Mexicans had not really wanted an emperor.

The French soldiers are returning home! We will have our own government again!

Viva Juarez!

I do not know what will happen here. You must sail for Europe!

Louis Napoleon is leaving here with no one to help you.

I will talk to him! I will talk to the Pope! Someone must send help!

Juarez, their commander, led the Mexicans in battle. They took back their country from the French.

Viva Juarez!

But no one would, or could, help Maximilian.

Viva Mexico!

Maximilian died before a firing squad.* This ended the French dream of a lasting American colony.

FIRE!

* group of men who put people to death by shooting them

In the same year, 1867, Secretary Seward had a visitor.

The Russian ambassador*, Edward de Stoeckl, to see you, sir.

Well, show him in!

After the greetings, Stoeckl made an off

Our land in Alaska is too far from Russi The cost of protecting and using it is too great. We would like to sell it to the United States.

If we can agree on a price I will take the matter to Congress.

The price, $7,200,000, was less than two cents an acre for half a million square miles. Congress agreed. But some Americans did not.

What do you think of "Seward's Folly"?

The icebox, you mean? Alaska? Nothing but a frozen waste-land.

The Indian slaves in Alaska were set free when it became American land. They carved a wooden statue.

It is Abraham Lincoln, the Great Emancipator!**

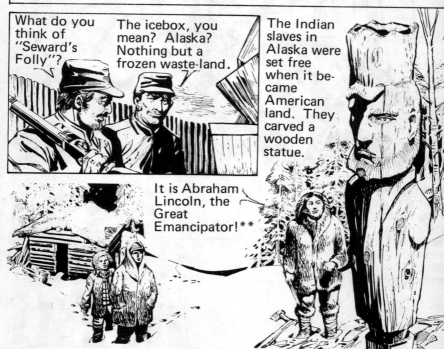

* someone who represents his own country to the government of another

** a title given to President Lincoln; it means someone who has set people free

In 1897, gold was found there. To reach it, people had to cross Chilkoot Pass.

'ithin five years, $100,000,000
orth of gold was mined!

Navy bases were soon set up. Today in the air age, some important air bases are there.

Soon a pipeline will cross Alaska, bringing much-needed oil to continental United States.

and other minerals have been found in Alaska. Now "Seward's lly" is a rich country, and the forty-ninth state of the Union.

ther events also helped America to become a world power. They ook place thousands of miles away, in the middle of the Pacific cean, on the Hawaiian Islands.

th the
nate*
I the
ple
the
waiian
ands
re friend-
Ameri-
ships
nd these
bors
d places
stop for
plies.

e usual weather

About 1820, American missionaries*
came to the Islands to start churches
and schools.

Most Hawaiians
became Christians.

These are the children
of the wealthy. Some-
day we hope to have
schools for all Hawaiian
children.

It is not right! This school te
our children the ways of the
Haoles** and the worship of
their God!

The God of the Missionaries
is the true God! Our old
gods lost their powers long
ago!

More and more people came to Hawaii. In 1842 there was
frightening news.

A British ship is in the
harbor. Its guns are
aimed at Honolulu.
They are trying
to take over
the Kingdom
of Hawaii.

My mother the
queen will neve
give in!

But there was
no defense
against the
British guns.
The Hawaiian
flag was taken
down. The
British flag
was raised.

* people who go to a new land to teach the people about God

** strangers

Judd, an American
sionary, was chief
iser to the Hawaiian
en.

For five months the
British ruled Hawaii.
Then another British
ship sailed into the
harbor.

In the schoolroom,
Mrs. Cooke talked to
her class again.

ve written about
to the English.
ve sent it by secret
senger to Queen
toria.

There is wonderful news!
Queen Victoria has or-
dered that Hawaii be
given back to the
Hawaiians. The queen
will rule again!

r this, American
sionaries continued to
the Hawaiian queen.

Hawaii must have
a constitution*
and elections. Land
should be divided
among all the
people.

But my people
do not know
about these
things!

ten set of laws

This proved to be true. Owning land for the first time, the Hawaiians sold it for a few dollars. Soon there were large plantations of sugar cane. More Americans arrived, and many Hawaiians married them. The islands soon wanted closer ties to the United States. They also wanted the same form of government. Plans were made to do this.

In 1893, American marines came ashore from the *U.S.S. Boston.*

After a peaceful revolution* Queen Liliuokalani gave up her throne.

Once again the Hawaiian flag was lowered. This time the flag of the United States went up.

We have done what we believe to be for the best. You must accept it, or there will be fighting.

I will give in to the United States.

The new government asked to be added to the United States. In 1898, this was done. Finally, in 1959, Hawaii became the fiftieth state of the Union.

* a change of government brought about either peacefully or through civil war

851 the Secretary of
e, Daniel Webster,
ed to Commodore
thew Perry of the
. Navy.

r more than 200
ars, Japan has been
sed to the rest of the
rld. I want you to
to open the door
Americans!

s, sir!

You will try to
get help for
sailors ship-
wrecked in Japan.
You will try to
open their ports
to ships which
need supplies.
And we would
like to have them
open trade with us.

You will lead
the largest
American
fleet* ever
sent to the
Far East.
But your job
is peaceful!
Fighting is to
be used only to
defend yourselves.

I under-
stand,
sir!

e "largest fleet" was two steamships
d two sailing boats. They looked
all in the Great China Sea.

p of ships

rry got the Japanese to allow him to
ng a group ashore. The Japanese
ilt a special place to receive them.

er, Perry gave
Japanese
hy gifts. Their
rite was a
ll steam train.

Japan was open to
attack, but we sought
only trade and friend-
ship. In 1854, a treaty
was signed opening two
ports to Americans.
Later we were allowed
to send an ambassador.
Japan learned about
modern inventions very
quickly. Within fifty
years, Japan would fight
wars against Russia and
China.

Cuba, an island off the Florida coast, had belonged to Spain since 1492. Its people had become slaves and suffered a great deal. In the 1890s, many Americans wanted to fight Spain to free Cuba.

Grover Cleveland, the president, was visited by a group of men from Congress.

Mr. President, we have decided to declare war on Spain.

There will be no war while I am president! I am the head of the army and navy, and I will not let them fight!

In 1897, William McKinley was elected president. Cleveland gave him some advice.

One of your greatest problems will be keeping us out of a war with Spain.

War is the last thing I want for this country! In the Civil War, I saw the dead pile up.

President Polk tried to buy Cuba from Spain. Buchanan tried it too! Even Thomas Jefferson saw that Cuba should belong to us. But war is not the answer.

lking things over, that is
e way. But there is so
ich sympathy for Cuba...

And so many un-true stories in the press!

God help me to stay out of it!

Exactly! You may be forced into war.

n D. Long was made Secretary of
e navy, with Theodore Roosevelt
help him.

ke young Roosevelt, John.
t he tends to stir things
too much! I depend on
u to keep him quiet.

I'll do my best.

Roosevelt was sent to look over a torpedo boat,* under repair after an accident.

Great! Bully!

ip that can fire large bullet-shaped bombs underwater

Roosevelt sent in his report.

Torpedo boats must run great risks. It is more important that officers handle them with daring than that they should be kept unscratched!

Sir, this hardly sounds like the usual navy report!

Would you say this shows a new spirit in the navy?

It shows my feeling that we must have a *better* navy!

Roosevelt learned that not enough money was set aside to train nav men in target practice. He ordered that nearly a million dollars be spent for this.

Good! They're improving! Keep up the practice!

...eodore, we must not waste ...nuch money shooting ...o the sea.

Sir, we have a new type of gun. The men must learn how to use it. The only shots that count are the ones that hit!

...a talk at the Naval War ...llege in Newport, he ...ked for a stronger navy.

Being ready for war is the best way to keep the peace. It is too late to prepare for war when the time of peace has passed!

...or years Cuban guerrillas* had been ...ghting the Spaniards. Some were led ...y General Garcia.

In return, the Spaniards brought in General Weyler to rule.

...ll over the island, ...e will burn the ...gar mills.

So. They burn the mills. We will burn the cane fields!

...all groups who fight against larger armies; they often use surprise attacks or raids ...her than open war.

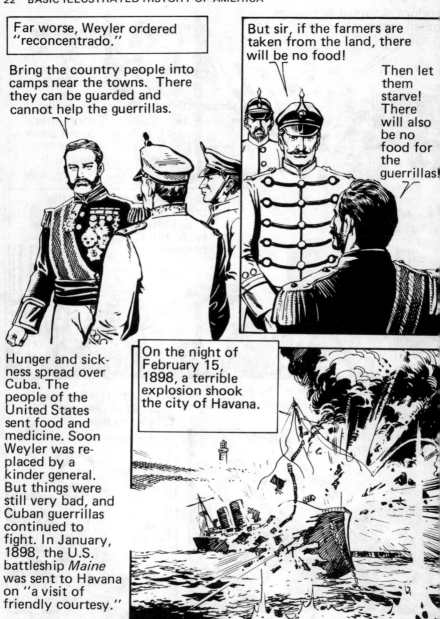

Far worse, Weyler ordered "reconcentrado."

Bring the country people into camps near the towns. There they can be guarded and cannot help the guerrillas.

But sir, if the farmers are taken from the land, there will be no food!

Then let them starve! There will also be no food for the guerrillas!

Hunger and sickness spread over Cuba. The people of the United States sent food and medicine. Soon Weyler was replaced by a kinder general. But things were still very bad, and Cuban guerrillas continued to fight. In January, 1898, the U.S. battleship *Maine* was sent to Havana on "a visit of friendly courtesy."

On the night of February 15, 1898, a terrible explosion shook the city of Havana.

The battleship *Maine* had blown up in Havana harbor.

Washington,
rly in the morn-
g of February 16,
hts burned in the
vy department.
essengers hurried
rough the quiet
y.

Secretary
ong's house.

At dawn, the president was awakened.

What is it?

Sir, an important message from Secretary Long.

Although he had a house guest, Myron T. Herrick, the president was late for breakfast.

There's bad news. The *Maine* exploded in Havana harbor. She sank with more than 250 of her men.

You're late, sir! And you look very stern today.

God,
! What
used

No one knows. But we will study it right away. The country must not fight back until the truth is known!

But the people wanted to fight!

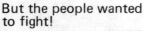

Extral! *Maine* blown up! Hundreds of sailors killed!

We could send 600 Sioux Indians to scalp the Spanish!

How abc
a crowd
Indian
fighters,
under Cc
nel Buffa
Bill Cod

Isn't it terrible? Does it mean war?

Of course it means war! Would we let Spain get away with this?

Remember the *Maine!* That's our motto.

The U. S. Pacific ships were at anchor in Hong Kong harbor. One day when Secretary Long was away, Roosevelt sent a message to the commander.

Commodore Dewey went to work.

To Dewey, Hong Kong, China. Keep full of coal. If war begins, see that the Spanish ships do not leave the coast of Asia. We will fight in the Philippine Islands!

Order more gunpowder. Get coal from every-where...try Wales, too. And I want all the charts, maps, everything we have on the Philippines.

white paint
t be covered
gray.

On April 24, 1898, Dewey
received the message he
had waited for.

War has begun
between the
United States
and Spain!
We will go at
once to the
Philippines
to fight the
Spanish!

vey had four fighting ships, one gunboat, and three supply ships.
ropean navy officers in Hong Kong had been making bets to
vey's officers. They believed the Americans would be defeated
the Spanish. But the little group sailed with great hope. Three
hts later they lay off Manila Bay.

l take a chance on underwater
ines. But we haven't the armor
fight against their coast-defense
ns.

We must enter the harbor in
darkness. No lights except
a small guiding light on each
ship.

In the blackout, Dewey on the *Olympia* led the way. Suddenly soot in the smokestack of the *McCulloch* caught fire! Soon from Corregidor a signal rocket rose into the sky.

It has taken them a long time to wake up!

At six o'clock, the Spanish opened the battle.

Sixteen merchant ships at anchor, sir, and eleven enemy warships.

And, of course, the coast defense guns behind them.

With the ship's captain, Charles Gridley, beside him, Dewey watched as his ships drew closer.

Now! You may fire when you are ready, Gridley.

though the Spanish had more ships, the Americans had
re guns and were better shooters.

The Spanish fought bravely. But at 12:30 P.M., their ships sunk or in flames, they surrendered. There were 167 Spanish dead, 250 wounded. Dewey only had seven men wounded. The Americans were in control of Manila Bay.

ile Dewey had prepared for
r in Hong Kong, Washington
epared too. The president
ited for a report on the *Maine*.

The report arrived on March 24. McKinley talked with his cabinet.

. President.
ngress has
ted fifty
llion dollars
r your use
the national
fense!

I still hope for peace, but we must prepare for war.

The navy divers found signs of outside damage. The shot must have set off the ship's own magazines.*

ices where ammunition is stored.

Nothing to show who shot at the *Maine?*

Nothing at all. It could even have be a rebel, hoping to cause trouble for Spain.

It did indeed cause trouble for Spain. Senator Henry Cabot Lodge of Massachusetts gave a report.

I believe the *Maine* was blown up by a government mine. I'm sure the Spanish had a high-ranking officer in charge.

Both the people and Congress agreed with Lodge.

Due in part to Roosevelt, the navy was ready for action. Dewey won the first victory of the war. Secretary of War Alger called for more soldiers.

I am raisin three caval units. I w make you an officer of the Firs U. S. Volu teer Caval

No, sir. I've had too little training. Make Leonard Wood the officer, and I'll serve under him.

Very well, if that's the way you want it. You'll be lieuten colonel.

* soldiers on horseback

nard
od, an
y doctor,
 both
ical and
tary skill.

I'm off
to San
Antonio
where
we'll
train.

I've ordered
a uniform
from New
York, a horse
from Texas,
and a dozen
pairs of eye-
glasses! I'll
join you as soon
as I can!

What sort of men
have you lined up?

Harvard men:
football players
and tennis players.
From the West,
Indians and Indian
fighters, cowboys,
sheriffs. They're
a good lot, sir!

he people of San Antonio were
terested in the odd group of
en, especially the cowboys.

By the time Roosevelt
arrived, a large sign was
hanging near the station.

ave you
en the
test group
f "Teddy's
errors"?

THIS WAY
TO ROOSEVELT
ROUGH RIDER
CAMP

I've seen
'em and
heard
'em!
Those
men are
rough
riders!

The army, under the command of General Shafter, was to ship out from Tampa, Florida.

But somehow, by June 22, 16,000 men were off the Cuban coast near Santiago.

Tell Alger that the troops are arriving without blankets, tents, uniforms, arms, ammunition, even without food! And we are very short of ships!

The Spaniards are reported to have 80,000 soldiers in Cuba. There are 36,000 on this eastern coast.

They'll attack us during the landing!

There was no way to land the animals. They were pushed overboard so they would swim to shore.

The men rode in lifeboats. At least two of them overturned.

on the shore
e were no
niards to be
nd. The
erican flag
raised as the
iers cheered.

Shafter made his plans known.

We will move to Santiago and attack it from land. The navy will blockade the harbor, catching the Spaniards between the forces.

tween the Americans and Santiago, the Spaniards had dug nches and placed barbed wire on the nearby hills. The nericans were stopped by enemy fire.

We must take that hill, boys. Forward! CHARGE!

With a cheer, the Rough Riders and soldiers of the black Ninth Cavalry followed Roosevelt up San Juan Hill.

They met a barbed-wire fence. Black soldiers rushed forward under fire from a Spanish fort.

The battle was fierce. Again and again Roosevelt's men charged the fort. Finally the Americans won a victory.

The negro soldiers saved that fight.

Those men are all right!

e American soldiers closed in on Santiago. Part of the Spanish
y was blocked in the harbor by the American Atlantic ships.
ing to escape, the Spanish ships were destroyed by the
ericans.

July 16, the Spanish
eral Torel surrendered
tiago to General Shafter.
e fight for Cuba was nearly
er.

On July 25, General Miles and
a group of Americans lay off
the coast of Puerto Rico.

There it is. It's the
only Spanish land left
in the western
hemisphere. We will
take it and end the
Spanish dream of
colonies in the
new world.

Miles landed on the south coast with 5,000 men. Within twenty days, the American flag was raised over the Puerto Rican capital, San Juan.

Commodore Dewey was on the other side of the world in the Philippines. News of his victory pleased and surprised people in the United States.

What's the parade for?

Celebrating Dewey's victory in the Philippines.

That's great! But where are the Philippines?

Well... somewhere in the Pacific, I think.

Now we've got colonies like the other great countries.

President McKinley and Secretary Long talked together.

I've sent Dewey our congratulations. I told him that he was to be made an admiral.*

Good! And by the way... just where are the Philippines?

*the highest rank in the navy

On August 12, less than four months after the war had begun, the United States and Spain agreed to end the fighting. But the peace treaty was put off by the problem of the Philippines.

Cuba will be free. Puerto Rico will be taken care of by the United States. But the more I learn about the Philippines, the less I know what to do about them.

Senator Lodge has a large group who thinks we should keep them.

But the spirit that led this country into the war was not to gain more land. We wanted to help people who needed help.

Yet there are more than 7,000 different islands in the Philippines. There are many different races, tribes, religions. They are not prepared to govern themselves.

We can hardly return them to Spain!

No, no! And we can't turn them over to any European power or to Japan. There seems but one thing to do, and that is to keep them!

The Treaty of Paris was signed on December 10, 1898. By it, the United States became the owner of Puerto Rico, the Philippines, and the island of Guam. They paid Spain $20,000,000.

In Cuba the battles were over, but army men were still dying.

Sir, our men are becoming very sick! There are many new cases of fever and many deaths.

General Shafter called his officers together.

Malaria and dysentery* are bad, but the real problem is yellow fever. No one knows the cause. It seems to spread in the night air.

Unless this army is moved out, everyone will die!

The army was moved to the mainland except for the soldiers under General Wood. But the yellow fever stayed. In 1900 it spread widely among the Cubans.

We must end this fever once and for all! I am sending Dr. Walter Reed to study it.

Reed and his men arrived in Cuba.

As you know, sir, we have burned all clothes, bedding, everything that has touched people with the disease. But this has never stopped its spread.

Yes, Major...

*two diseases which spread rapidly in crowded living spaces

think it may be
read by the bite
a mosquito. I
nt to use some
en in a test.

u may have what-
r you need!

must save them!
ve never known
braver men!

First, some men
slept in the
pajamas and beds
of men who had
died from yellow
fever.

Sir, twenty
nights have
passed. We
are still all
healthy.

Thank
God
for
that!

Reed asked for more
men for another
test. Private John
Kissenger, a hospital
aide, stepped forward.

You will be kept in a
screened room with
many mosquitoes. You
know that I believe they
carry the disease?

Yes,
sir! But
I will do
it, sir!

Another man, John Moran,
also helped with the test.
In a few days, both men
became very ill.

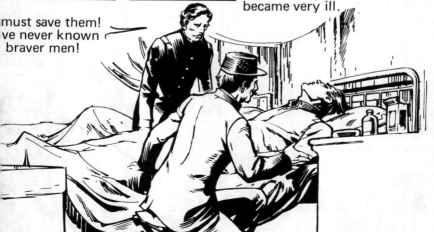

Both men got better. Walter Reed had good news for General Wood and for the world.

Good news, sir. Yellow fever is spread by a mosquito. Control the mosquitoes and you control yellow fever!

Wonderful news, Major!

Send out an order to spread oil on all places where mosquitoes can breed.

At onc[e] sir.

By 1901, there was not a sin[gle] case of yellow fever in Havar[a]. One of the greatest ills of the tropics* had been conquered

Other things were needed to make Cuba once more a fit place to live. The army fed the hungry, and cared for the sick. Roads, schools, public buildings were built or repaired. Wood also took steps to set up a government.

In November, 1900, the Cubans voted for delegates to a constitutional convention.**

VOTO (AQUI!)

Look, littl[e] one! Your father has fought against the Spanish fo[r] a free Cuba[.] Now he vo[tes] for one!

*the lands farthest from the North and South Poles; places that are always very hot
** a meeting held to draw up a constitution, a set of rules for a new government

e United States asked for several favors. We wanted a navy at
antanamo. We wanted the right to keep order in Cuba when
as needed.

neral Wood told the Cuban
ders the feelings of the
ited States.

In May, 1902, the United
States army left, and Cuba
began to rule itself.

In 1934, by Cuba's demand,
America's right to keep order
was ended.

retary of War Alger left the
inet. And Elihu Root got a
ne call.

president
es you
ecome
retary
Var.

Thank him, but I
cannot do it. I
know nothing about
war. I know nothing
about the army.

President McKinley says
that he is not looking
for anyone who knows
anything about war.
He needs a lawyer to
direct the government
of these Spanish
islands. You are the
lawyer he wants.

Elihu Root accepted the job. After doing his homework, he talked with the president.

The Puerto Rican people are poor. There are too many people, too little good land to feed them.

What steps should we take to help?

Take away our soldiers, set up a new government and feed the people!

Shortly afterward, the island was hit by a hurricane.*

The crops were ruined. President McKinley asked for money to help the people. Many Americans helped. War ships sailed to Puerto Rico with tons of supplies. Root gave them food from the army.

* a great storm with high winds, heavy rain, and floods

...he United States was worried
...ore about the Puerto Ricans'
...ed for food than for a good
...vernment. But we had to help
...that area, too.

...hey should be a "crown-
...olony."

We made some mistakes. But
in 1917 the Puerto Ricans
were made American citizens.

What does
it mean—
we are
now
United
States
citizens?

For one thing, we
can go to the
United States as
people who live
there—not as
visitors!

Yes...a voting group elected
by the people themselves,
but with a governor named
by myself as President.

...ce then, Puerto Ricans have given many things to the
...nerican people.

...se Ferrer is a great
...tor, director and
...oducer. He was
...rn in Santurce...

Two baseball players
are Orlando Cepeda
and Roberto Clemente.

And millions of Puerto Rican workers
have come to live in the United
States. They have taught us much
about the Spanish way of life.

In 1948, there was an important election.

For the first time in 450 years, Puerto Ricans will elect their own governor!

The man elected was Luis Munoz Marin.

I am proud to be elected. I am happy that my fellow Puerto Ricans have voted to become a commonwealth.*

The constitution of the Commonwealth of Puerto Rico went into effect on July 25, 1952.

In 1900, McKinley had talked about the Philippines with Elihu Root.

Two years ago Admiral Dewey said the Filipino rebels would not fight us. General Miles keeps saying they are conquered. But we still have a large army fighting in the Philippines!

I am sending General MacArthur to take charge.

General MacArthur spoke to the people.

Wherever the American flag goes, the idea of freedom goes.

But the Filipino rebel leader Aguinaldo and hi guerrillas continued to f

* a group of people who have their own government

en Colonel
nston had a
n. With
mbers of
ibe loyal
he Ameri-
s, he landed
r Aguinaldo's
ing place.

I have sent a
message to
Aguinaldo
that we
bring you
as a captive!

Good!

or days
ey
arched
rough the
ngle
ward
guinaldo's
deout,
ting as if
unston had
en
ptured.

utside Aguinaldo's hiding place there was
fight, and Aguinaldo was captured before
knew what was happening.

The fighting ended.
Aguinaldo became
a citizen of the
American Philip-
pines. A govern-
ment was set
up. Under Ameri-
can rule the
Filipinos improved
their schools and
government. On
July 4, 1946,
they became a
free country.

In 1900 McKinley was elected president. Theodore Roosevelt became vice-president.

On September 6, 1901, the president greeted the crowd at the Pan-American Exposition at Buffalo. Suddenly a man with his hand covered drew near.

Pulling off the handkerchief, Leon Czolgosz fired two bullets.

Within eight days McKinley had died and Roosevelt was president. His first message to Congress was read on December 6.

To protect our interests in both the Atlantic and Pacific oceans, a canal joining the two must be built.

r since Columbus, people
e looked for a water
te to the Pacific. The
nish talked of a
al. The French spent
ions trying to build

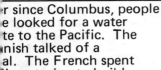

If any-
body can
do it,
it's Teddy
Roosevelt!

The French canal company
had valuable land in Panama.
They would sell it to us if
we built a canal there. But
Panama was part of Colombia,
and Colombia would not
agree. French agents wanted
them to separate from
Colombia. In November,
1903, the people of Panama
finally broke away from
them. A new flag was
raised over Panama City.

o days
r the
ited
tes
ognized

ublic
Panama.
retary

ed a
aty.

This
treaty
gives your country
the right to build
a canal.

Indeed,
yes!

This proved to
be the worst
treaty the
U. S. ever signed.
But it *did* allow
the building of
the Panama Canal.

onel William
gas was the
dical officer
harge. The
at enemies were
aria and yel-
fever.

nust have ditches
arry off the
er, and oil for
ying.

He used as
much as
50,000 gal-
lons of oil
a month.
But Gorgas
turned the
canal zone
into a health
resort.

Colonel George Goethals was chief engineer* of this huge job.

It will need the biggest locks in the world. The Gatun Dam will be the largest dam. Gatun lake will be the largest man-made body of water.

In 1906, Roosevelt him came to see the canal.

It's bully!

On August 14, 1914, The S.S. *Ancon* made history. It was the first ship to pass through the Panama Canal. Everything worked perfectly.

From the first, the canal was a success. But the people of Panama did not like the powers given to the United States by treaty. In 1964 they broke into the Canal Zone. A new treaty was worked out, but Panama is still not happy.

By 1980, if not sooner, the canal will be overcrowded. A new canal is being planned. It will be built in a new place at sea level (without locks) and will use atomic power.

* a person who plans roads, buildings, canals, and bridges

his first message to Congress,
osevelt also talked about
big corporations* — the
sts.

ey must be watched
controlled. Those
o sell in other states
uld allow a full study
their business practices.

Later he gave orders to his
Attorney General, Philander
Knox.

Begin a lawsuit**
against the Northern
Securities Company.
They have not
obeyed the Sherman
Anti-trust law.

Yes, I agree.
They have put
many small
companies out
of business.

The railroads had joined together
in the Northwest. The courts voted
against the company. Soon
lawsuits were brought against
many such companies.

osevelt asked for a study of
meat and food companies.
overnment man reported.

e stockyards are terrible.
the companies that can
food are using colorings
other things that are not
d for people.

A candy-maker who added
pieces of bone to his coco-
nut bars said, "It doesn't
hurt the kids. They like
it!"

That's
too much!

And so Congress passed the
Pure Food and Drug Act.

mpany owned by many people
urt action which might end in a trial

In 1902, the coal miners took their problems to John Mitchell, United Mine Workers' president.

Our year's pay is $560, and we don't even get that! They take money out for these company houses. And we have to buy at the company store.

And we all know mine work is dangerous.

We work ten to twelve hours a day.

I know very well, men. There's nothing to do but call a strike.

140,000 miners went on strike. The owners would not even talk to Mitchell. All summer, no coal was mined.

The whole country was worried. In October, Roosevelt called Mitchell and the mine owners to the White House for a talk.

Schools are closing for lack of coal. The price is so high that most people cannot buy it. I can't settle your argument, but you can do something about it.

Open the mines, go back to work, and let me help to settle your problem.

I accept your help, sir.

Never! Speak the owners, w not accept.

Roosevelt was ready to order a group of soldiers to open the mines. But the mine owners finally agreed to give the men a ten percent increase in their pay. Soon they were back at work.

ce the country began, no one had thought much about
land. Roosevelt knew that it must be cared for.

nder the Reclamation Act
1902, great dams were
uilt in the West to water
e dry land.

A Forest Service was begun.
Roosevelt's greatest supporter,
Gifford Pinchot, was in
charge.

Many people want the forests
for their own profit.

We will
save
some
of them
for the
country!

ore than 3,000,000 acres of
y land were made useful.

Roosevelt changed the Na-
tional Forest area from
43,000,000 to 194,000,000
acres.

ve new
tional
rks were
gun.
e was
e Grand
anyon.

ty-
e wild
d refuges* and
o national game
serves* were
up. One was
t for buffalo.

aces where wild animals can live safely

The wave of change that swept through Roosevelt's term of office continued. The new president, William Howard Taft, and Woodrow Wilson, who followed him, made many good changes.

On election night, the Wilsons waited for the voting results at their home in New Jersey. A message was handed to Mrs. Wilson.

Wilson had been a teacher as well as the president of Princeton University. Now the students formed a parade and came to celebrate.

I have no feeling of victory. I know that I have an important job to do.

She moved to Wilson's side.

My dear, I want to be the first to congratulate you. You are the second Democratic president since the Civil War.

He spoke to Congress on April 7, 1913.

We made the American people a promise...of a New Freedom. I call upon you to help this come true!

With Wilson leading, Congress acted.

This will lower the tariff rates. It's the first true tariff reform since the Civil War!

And added to the tariff act is an income tax. It was allowed by the sixteenth amendment* to the Constitution.

Samuel Gompers, president of the AFL, liked a law that was passed in 1914.

The Federal Reserve Act changed the nation's banking system. But not everyone liked it.

The Federal Trade Commission and the Clayton Anti-trust Act are good. Thank you.

I say to you, this bill is not legal!

But it was passed. It was soon called the most important money law made since Alexander Hamilton's day.

*change that makes something better

In August, 1914, World War I broke out in Europe. Germany moved into Belgium to attack France. Austria - Hungary and Turkey joined Germany. England and Russia stood by France.

A war between great powers? Not in this modern age! We must stay out of it—or every change we have made will be lost.

On August 4, Wilson announc[ed] that America would not enter the war.

The United States must be neutral* in fact as well as in name.

England decided to block ships going to Germany. Her navy stopped neutral ships and searched them for war goods. Whenever they were found, they were taken. This angered Americans, but no lives were lost and the goods taken were paid for. But Germany did more than this.

On February 4, 1915, the emperor of Germany made an announcement.

All waters around England are in a war zone. Any merchant ship found there will be destroyed!

On May 1, an American ship was torpedoed and sunk. On May 7, the British ship *Lusitania* was torpedoed off the Irish coast. It sank in fifteen minutes.

1,198 people died. 128 of them were Americans.

* not taking either side in a war or argument

By law, if a warship takes or destroys a merchant ship, it must get the people to safety. But the German submarines* strike without warning and kill all on board!

I will tell this to Germany in the strongest terms. But I will not be pushed into war! We are not ready. The people are divided in their feelings. I hate war!

Germany thought that America would not fight because she was weak. Becoming certain that America would not fight, Germany announced a submarine war. She sank many neutral ships, including American ships. Wilson spoke to Congress on April 2, 1917.

The night before, he walked the floors of the White House.

The next evening, he asked Congress to make war on Germany.

What else can I do? Is there anything else I can do?

. Germany has ced the war on the United ates.

It is a fearful thing to lead this great peaceful people into war. We shall fight for freedom, and for the rights and liberties of small nations.

underwater ships

Across Europe, on the fields of the Western front,* the fighting went on.

In the battle of Verdun, the French stopped a German advance—and lost 350,000 men.

In the battle of the Somme, a new weapon, the tank, was used. The French lost 200,000 men, the British 400,000. They won only a few miles of land.

After the United States entered the war, Congress at once passed a Selective Service Act.**

All men between the ages of 21 and 31 years of age will wait for a call to military duty...

* a war zone

** the draft law, which made many young men soldiers

On June 27, 1918, Secretary of War Baker drew the first number for the draft.

ur only other draft call, uring the Civil War, aused riots. Will our eople accept one today?

I think they will prove loyal, Mr. President.

To the joy and pride of America, the draft was carried out with ease. Soon 4,000,000 men were drafted. About half reached the fighting line.

fter several months training camps, e troops were aded onto ips for e voyage France.

They sailed in secret. No American ships were lost to submarines.

General John J. Pershing was given command of the U. S. Army. In 1918, he had bad news.

The Italian army has been smashed. And the Russians, after many German defeats, have left the war.

Leaving the Germans free to move many more soldiers to the French front?

Yes! In the spring the Germans will begin a great attack. Only fresh soldiers can save us. Will the Americans arrive in time?

It takes time to train soldiers. There are only 250,000 here now. I will push for one million by spring.

In March, the German leaders had a plan.

The Americans are getting ready for war. We must strike now before they come to help the French and English.

I will order an attack all along the line!

The German soldiers swept forward in a great attack.

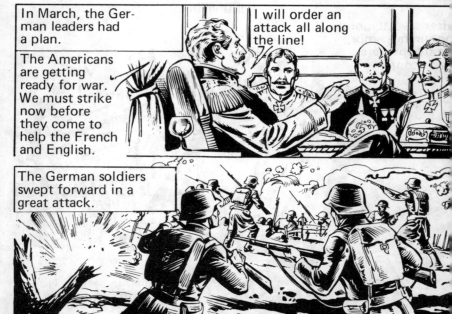

...e Germans took 3,000 square miles before they were stopped.
...t American soldiers were reaching Europe at the rate of
...,000 men a day.

...great attack was planned in
...hich 896,000 Americans
...ok part.

The kaiser* left his throne, and the Germans asked for peace. On November 11, 1918, President Wilson told the good news.

...he head of the German government
...ruce; stopping the fighting of a war

The Paris Peace Conference was held to draw up the treaty. The "Big Four" leaders of their countries were: Clemenceau of France, Lloyd George of Great Britain, Orlando of Italy, and President Wilso

We must put away all weapons of war!

It is Germany who must put aside her weapons.

She must give up her colonies. The Rhineland * should be taken away and given to France.

Wilson refused to agree to some of the demands of England and France. While it was not as strong as these countries had wanted, the treaty was, of course, too harsh to suit Germany.
What saved the group was the start of a League of Nations for settling future problems.

If Italy is not given Fiume, I will leave this conference.

But in America a strange feeling was growing. Could it be that Wilson's own country would turn down the League? Senator Lodge spoke against it.

Wilson spoke to his doctor, Dr. Grayson.

I must travel through the country. I must go to the people and tell them of the need for the Leagu

If we join, we in America must give up in part our freedom. We will have to subject our own will to the will of other nations.

Mr. Preside you can't You're wo Your healt won't stan

He gave President Wilson an anti-League paper signed by thirty-seven senators.

But Wilson went. For th next three weeks he travelled many miles, speaking two or three times a day.

* a part of Germany west of the Rhine River

Pueblo, Colorado, he became
y sick. He was hurried back
the White House.

e was never really well again.

On March 19, 1920, he was
told that the Senate had
voted 49 to 35 against the
Treaty of Versailles.

I feel like going
to bed and
staying there.

June, Wilson was visited by the
emocratic candidate* for
resident, James M. Cox, and the
andidate for vice-president,
ranklin D. Roosevelt.

r. President, we are a million
ercent with you...and that means
e League of Nations!

Thank
you
very
much.

Wilson had spoken
about the future.

If the United States does
not join the League of
Nations, there will be
a breakup of the world.
It will be much more
than a war...

Dying in 1924, he did
not live to see the
start of World War II, less
than twenty years later.
★★★★

t the Republican candidate,
arren Harding, was elected, and
e United States did not join the
eague of Nations.

meone who hopes to be elected to an office

Words to know

admiral	guerrillas
amendment	kaiser
armistice	lawsuit
candidate	neutral
commonwealth	revolution
constitutional	Rhineland
emperor	Selective Service Act
firing squad	The Great Emancipator
fleet	torpedo boat
front	tropics

Questions

1. While the book does not really say so, Napoleon had a very good reason for making Maximilian the emperor of Mexico. Can you tell what that reason was?

2. What happened to Maximilian?

3. Why did Russia offer to sell Alaska to the United States? Was it a good bargain for us?

4. For what three reasons did Daniel Webster send Commodore Perry to Japan?

5. Why were the people of America so eager for a war with Spain?

6. What name was given to Theodore Roosevelt's soldiers in the Spanish-American War?

7. Dr. Walter Reed was able to stop the spread of yellow fever in Cuba. How did he stop it?

8. In the world of business, what is a "trust"? Why was President Roosevelt against trusts?

9. Name some of the things that President Theodore Roosevelt did to help care for American land.

10. President Woodrow Wilson tried to keep the United States out of World War I. How did we finally get into it?

Match the following people and objects with the things they are famous for:

1. Lloyd George
2. torpedo boat
3. George Goethals
4. Commodore Perry
5. tank
6. income tax
7. Admiral Dewey
8. William H. Seward
9. Clemenceau
0. Liliuokalani

a. spoke for France at the Paris Peace Conference

b. weapon first used in World War I

c. made possible by the sixteenth amendment

d. spoke for England at the Paris Peace Conference

e. chief engineer of the Panama Canal

f. American officer who helped open Japan to trade

g. last queen of Hawaii

h. important weapon used in Spanish-American War

i. bought Alaska from Russia for the U.S.

j. famous American officer in Spanish-American War

Complete the following sentences

. Before the United States got into World War I, England and France were helped by _____ .

2. Germany was joined by Austria-Hungary and _____ during World War I.

3. The Germans thought that America would not join World War I because the country was _____ .

. President Wilson wanted the United States to join the _____ to settle future problems and prevent other wars.

. At the Paris Peace Conference ending World War I, America, France, Great Britain, and Italy were known as the " _____ " nations.